Original title:
Chill Beneath the Pines

Copyright © 2024 Swan Charm
All rights reserved.

Author: Paulina Pähkel
ISBN HARDBACK: 978-9916-79-867-6
ISBN PAPERBACK: 978-9916-79-868-3
ISBN EBOOK: 978-9916-79-869-0

Nature's Gentle Repose

In the hush of dawn's first light,
Birds begin their sweet refrain.
Leaves whisper secrets, soft and bright,
As the world awakens again.

Clouds drift lazily in the sky,
Casting shadows on the ground.
Butterflies in colors fly,
Nature's beauty all around.

Rivers murmur a soothing tune,
While flowers dance in gentle breeze.
Underneath the silver moon,
Time slows down, and worries cease.

Mountains stand with ancient grace,
Guardians of the tranquil scene.
In their arms, we all find space,
Where our hearts can wander free.

Stars emerge as day turns night,
Filling the heavens with their glow.
In this calm, we find delight,
Nature's peace forever flows.

A Canopy of Calm

Leaves whisper softly above,
The sun weaves through the green,
A gentle breeze lifts my heart,
Nature's grace, serene.

Shadows dance on the ground,
Time slows in this sacred space,
Here, worries drift away,
Peace wraps me in its embrace.

Birdsong fills the air,
Each note a soothing balm,
Under this vast canopy,
My spirit finds its calm.

Clouds drift lazily by,
Painting dreams in the blue,
Nature's beauty around me,
A moment to renew.

With each breath, I feel whole,
Grounded in the here and now,
Underneath these ancient trees,
I promise to take a vow.

Heartbeats in the Dappled Light

Sunbeams flicker on my skin,
As I wander through the glade,
Each step a silent rhythm,
In nature's serenade.

Dappled light on forest floor,
Patterns of gold and green,
A heartbeat in the stillness,
A union, pure and keen.

Rustling leaves tell a tale,
Of seasons softly past,
In these moments of wonder,
Eternal love is cast.

Mossy stones greet my feet,
Carpets of emerald plush,
In this world, my spirit dances,
Wrapped in the gentle hush.

With each pulse, I am found,
In the heart of the wild,
In the embrace of the trees,
Nature's cherished child.

Meditative Moments Under Boughs

Underneath the mighty oak,
I find solace and peace,
Branches stretch like arms of love,
In their shade, worries cease.

Butterflies flit on the breeze,
A flurry of colors bright,
In this tranquil sanctuary,
My soul takes flight.

The world slows to a hum,
With each inhaled breath I take,
Meditative moments linger,
In the stillness, I awake.

Sunset paints the sky gold,
As day softly yields to night,
Under boughs, I sit and reflect,
In this sacred light.

Whispered thoughts gently flow,
Like leaves that drift and fall,
In this meditative moment,
I am one with it all.

Echoes of the Pine Forest

Pine needles carpet the ground,
A fragrant, earthy scent,
Whispers of secrets untold,
In their shade, I am lent.

Tall sentinels watch above,
Standing strong through the years,
Their echoes fill the silence,
With the wisdom of ages.

Softly, the wind sings low,
Carrying stories divine,
Each rustle a reminder,
Of the threads that intertwine.

Ferns sway like gentle fans,
Caressing the ancient stone,
In the heart of the forest,
I find a home of my own.

As the sun begins to sink,
Gold spills through the pines,
In the echoes of this forest,
Peace and purpose aligns.

The Serenity of Earth's Breath

In the hush of dawn's caress,
Nature whispers soft and low,
Every leaf begins to dance,
With the rhythm of the flow.

Rivers sing their gentle tunes,
Mountains stand with steadfast grace,
Each moment holds a promise,
In this vast and open space.

Clouds drift by like whispered dreams,
Painting skies with shades of gold,
Time stands still, it seems to pause,
In this world of calm and bold.

Sunset spills a fiery hue,
Casting shadows long and deep,
In the twilight, all is clear,
Nature's secrets gently keep.

As night descends with quiet breath,
Stars awaken, one by one,
In the serenity of earth,
Life and love have just begun.

Pine Lullabies and Stillness

In the forest's gentle hold,
Pines sway softly in the breeze,
Their whispers tell old stories,
Of a time that seeks to please.

Beneath the shadows, silence reigns,
Mossy carpets cradle dreams,
Nature hums her lullabies,
Floating on the sunlit beams.

Squirrels dance among the boughs,
Chasing echoes, light and free,
Every rustle, every sigh,
A melody, a symphony.

As the sun begins to set,
Golden rays begin to fade,
The forest bathes in twilight's glow,
A tranquil world the light has made.

With the moon hanging high above,
Stars stitch patterns in the night,
Pine trees stand in quiet grace,
Guardians of this soft delight.

Moments of Silence in the Green Dome

Underneath the verdant arch,
Leaves create a whispered hush,
Every sound is amplified,
In the gentle, warming blush.

Sunlight dances through the trees,
Casting patterns on the ground,
In this sacred, green embrace,
Time slows down without a sound.

Wildflowers bloom in pure delight,
Colors splash like brush on canvas,
Nature's art, a quiet feat,
Beauty thrives in simple manners.

Birds high up begin to sing,
Echoing the calls of peace,
In this moment of stillness,
All our worries find release.

Here, in nature's soft embrace,
Life unfolds in shades of grace,
Moments linger, held in time,
In this dome, our spirits climb.

A Dance of Shadows and Light

In the glade where sunbeams play,
Shadows stretch and twist and turn,
Every corner held in light,
Where the heart begins to yearn.

Branches sway, a soft ballet,
As the wind begins to blow,
Nature partners with the dusk,
In a dance, both shy and slow.

Freed from worry, thoughts take flight,
In the play of dark and bright,
Every glimmer tells a tale,
Of the day's soft, fading light.

Crickets chirp their evening song,
Guiding stars to burst awake,
In this wondrous, peaceful scene,
Life reminds us what is at stake.

Hold this moment, breathe it in,
In the balance, find the bliss,
A dance of shadows, light, and heart,
Gracefully sealed with a kiss.

Green Canopies and Quiet Dreams

Underneath the leafy boughs,
Whispers dance on gentle air.
Dreams are born in emerald hues,
Resting softly without a care.

Mossy carpets cradle feet,
Tiny creatures scurry near.
Sunlight filters through the leaves,
Nature's lullaby we hear.

Breezes play with swaying limbs,
A symphony of rustling sounds.
Time surrenders to the calm,
In this sacred, timeless ground.

Each petal holds a secret thought,
Blossoms whisper, soft and light.
In the shade, our worries fade,
In the warmth of day and night.

Lost in dreams beneath the green,
Where life hums an endless rhyme.
Here we find our quiet peace,
In nature's arms, we pause time.

The Calm Amongst Tall Sentinels

Beneath the watchful giant trees,
Nature's guardians in the sky.
Silence drapes the forest floor,
Where secrets blend and shadows lie.

Rustling leaves tell ancient tales,
Of days gone by and paths unseen.
In the shade of mighty trunks,
A quiet heart finds solace green.

The breeze carries soft whispers,
A melody both sweet and rare.
Within this tranquil, sacred space,
A deep connection fills the air.

Misty dawns bring calm anew,
As sunlight breaks the sleepy night.
In the arms of tall sentinels,
We bask in their eternal light.

Walking slow on earthy trails,
Where time unfolds and peace prevails.
In this forest, life renews,
The calm amidst the tall, the true.

Secret Passages of the Timberland

Hidden paths between the trees,
Invite us to explore and roam.
Twisting trails where wild things hide,
In the heart of nature's home.

Branches weave a tapestry
Of shadows playing with the sun.
Each step reveals a mystery,
In the woodlands, we are one.

Softly through the thickets we tread,
Curiosity as our guide.
With every twist and turn we make,
New wonders bloom, old fears subside.

Birdsong fills the air with cheer,
A chorus echoing the green.
Here in the timberland's embrace,
Life reveals what has not been seen.

Through secret passages we flow,
Each turn a story softly spun.
Nature whispers in our ears,
In the wild, we feel at home.

Threads of Sunlight Through the Green

Golden beams filter through leaves,
Casting patterns on the ground.
Nature's brush strokes paint the scene,
Echoing a gentle sound.

Each ray a tale of warmth and light,
Illuminating paths we tread.
In the dance of shadow and sun,
Our weary thoughts are gently fed.

Lush canopies embrace the skies,
Breathing life into every space.
Within this vibrant, sacred world,
We find our bliss, a soft embrace.

Mornings bloom with hopeful grace,
As sunlight weaves through branches high.
Through every leaf, through every hue,
Life unfolds beneath the sky.

Endless threads of warmth and glow,
Wrap us in their golden seam.
In forests deep, our spirits soar,
Chasing after light, we dream.

Meditations in the Mossy Hollow

In the hollow where shadows play,
Moss wraps memories in green,
Whispers of nature softly sway,
Where silence fills the unseen.

Sunlight dapples through the leaves,
A dance of light and shade,
In stillness, the heart believes,
In dreams, the soul is laid.

Each breath carries the scent of earth,
Tender moss beneath my feet,
In this place, I sense my worth,
Every moment feels complete.

The rustling leaves, a gentle tune,
Echoes of time, sweet and slow,
Beneath the watchful, crescent moon,
In stillness, I come to know.

Peace resides in hidden glades,
Where footfalls whisper their intent,
The heart's unrest slowly fades,
In this mossy hollow, content.

Cool Breezes and Soft Shadows

Breezes cool beneath the trees,
Caressing skin with tender grace,
Shadows dance with playful ease,
In this tranquil, sacred space.

Leaves murmur secrets on the air,
Gentle whispers pass me by,
Each cool breath, a soothing prayer,
As clouds drift slowly in the sky.

Golden light spills through the boughs,
Painting patterns on the ground,
Nature's canvas softly bows,
In its beauty, I am found.

The soft rustle of the grass,
Reminds me of the day's sweet end,
In the twilight, moments pass,
As daylight and night blend.

The world holds still in this embrace,
Where time slows just enough to see,
Life unfolds with gentle grace,
In cool breezes, I am free.

Retreat to the Timbered Tranquility

In timbered halls of towering trees,
A sanctuary for the mind,
Nature's song whispers with ease,
In this retreat, peace I find.

Branches stretch like open arms,
Welcoming weary souls within,
Away from life's relentless charms,
Where stillness begins to spin.

Beneath the trunks, soft shadows lie,
A carpet woven from the past,
Here, the heart learns how to sigh,
In each moment, love is cast.

Songs of the forest fill the air,
Each note a balm to wandering hearts,
In the embrace of nature's care,
Every worry slowly departs.

Retreat into this sacred grove,
Where time holds no weight, nor chain,
In the timbered peace, I rove,
This tranquility is my gain.

Soft Earth and Swaying Boughs

On soft earth, where dreams can thrive,
I wander through the tranquil plain,
With each step, my spirit dives,
Embracing joy, releasing pain.

The boughs above begin to sway,
A symphony of nature's grace,
In their dance, I lose my way,
Finding solace in their embrace.

Birdsong flutters through the trees,
A melody both sweet and pure,
Inviting hearts to find the keys,
To unlock joy, forever sure.

The quiet earth knows all my fears,
And cradles me like gentle rain,
Here amidst the swaying gears,
Nature's touch can heal the pain.

Beneath the sky, so vast and bright,
With every breath, I'm drawn anew,
In swaying boughs, the world feels right,
Soft earth, my heart's eternal view.

Nature's Reclining Moment

Gentle streams flow by,
Whispers of soft grass,
Sunlight filters down,
In a serene dance.

Birds sing sweetly near,
Their melodies pure,
A tapestry woven,
In the light's allure.

Mountains stand majestic,
As guardians bold,
Cradling the valleys,
In their arms of gold.

Flowers sway gently,
Painting fields with cheer,
The scent of the earth,
Calms the wandering fear.

Time seems to linger,
In this sacred space,
Nature's embrace beckons,
With a tender grace.

Echoes of the Wind's Caress

Winds weave through the trees,
Whispers in the night,
Stories of the past,
Caught in silver light.

Leaves dance with passion,
In a carefree swirl,
Each gust of sweet air,
Makes the heart unfurl.

Voices of the wild,
Softly intertwine,
Carrying secrets,
In the evening's wine.

Mountains hold their breath,
In the stillness near,
Echoes of the wind,
Bring the past to hear.

In the dusky twilight,
Where dreams may reside,
The wind's caress lingers,
With nature as guide.

Under the Watchful Pines

Beneath tall pines standing,
Shadows gently play,
A carpet of kindness,
Blinks the sun's warm ray.

Branches stretch like arms,
Caressing the ground,
In this quiet haven,
Peace is truly found.

Squirrels dance with joy,
Chasing in the blue,
While the world above,
Shows its vivid hue.

Time flows like a river,
In this silent grove,
Nature's wise whispers,
Make the heart feel known.

Underneath the canopy,
Where dreams softly sigh,
The watchful pines shelter,
Every passing cry.

Hushed Conversations Among Sticks

Sticks lay in formation,
Stories etched in bark,
Roots tangle with silence,
As night begins to dark.

Breezes soft and light,
Carry whispers low,
Hushed conversations bloom,
Where only they know.

Crickets sing their song,
In a rhythmic charm,
Nature's subtle voice,
Keeps the night warm.

Moonlight spills like silk,
On the forest floor,
Casting dreams of wishes,
Opening the door.

In this gentle moment,
Under starlit sky,
Conversations linger,
As shadows drift by.

Languid Hours Among the Trees

In the shade where whispers dwell,
Time drifts slow, a gentle spell.
Leaves sway softly, dance in light,
In this peace, the world feels right.

Sunbeams trickle through the boughs,
Nature pauses, takes a bow.
Birds croon sweetly, echo wide,
In their songs, our hearts confide.

Moss carpets ground in shades of green,
A hidden world, serene, unseen.
Branches cradle weary souls,
While nature's breath, a hush, consoles.

Glimmers spark in twilight glow,
Dreams are born in ebb and flow.
Moments linger, time stands tall,
In this haven, we have it all.

Languid hours drip like honey,
Soft and sweet, both warm and funny.
Here we linger, lost in thought,
In every sigh, a solace sought.

Beneath a Shroud of Green

Beneath a shroud of emerald leaves,
Nature whispers, softly weaves.
Secret paths and hidden charms,
In this green, the spirit calms.

Sunlight filters, soft and warm,
Welcoming us with gentle charm.
Roots embrace the earth so tight,
In this realm, our dreams take flight.

Bird song greets the morning hours,
Awakening the sleeping flowers.
Petals blush with colors bright,
In this sanctuary of light.

Swaying grasses, soft and free,
Carry away our troubles, be.
In the rustling, joy is found,
Nature wraps us all around.

Beneath the green, our worries cease,
In every moment, find our peace.
Here, the heart learns how to mend,
In nature's arms, we transcend.

Nature's Sanctuary of Sighs

In the stillness, whispers sigh,
Nature's voice, a lullaby.
Every leaf and rustled sound,
Welcomes us to this safe ground.

Clouds drift lazily across the sky,
While the breeze carries forth our cry.
In this refuge, worries fade,
In the harmony we've made.

Streams murmur secrets, tales of old,
In their waters, dreams unfold.
Reflections shimmer on the surface,
In this peace, we find our purpose.

Mountains stand, a silent guard,
Protecting joys that we can't discard.
In their shadow, hope ignites,
As the stars emerge at night.

Nature's sighs, a soothing balm,
In this space, we feel the calm.
Breathing in the falls and highs,
We find our home in nature's sighs.

Shaded Dreams and Solitary Thoughts

In the shade where dreams take flight,
Solitary thoughts dance in light.
Beneath the canopy so wide,
In this silence, we confide.

Sunset paints a canvas bold,
With hues of red and glimmers gold.
Each moment cradled soft and slow,
In this serenity, we grow.

Whispers of the wind, so sweet,
Guide our hearts down this retreat.
Nature cradles, tender and wise,
As we weave beneath the skies.

Shadows stretch and softly blend,
In this quiet, we transcend.
Here, the world is far away,
In solitude, we choose to stay.

Shaded dreams, a tranquil sound,
In nature's heart, our truths abound.
Solitary paths we walk,
In silence, we find how to talk.

Under the Cool Canopy

Beneath the leaves, the shadows play,
Where whispers of the trees convey,
A gentle breeze, a soft caress,
In nature's arms, we find our rest.

The sunlight filters through the green,
Creating patterns, sights unseen,
A world of calm, where worries cease,
Under this canopy, we find peace.

The rustle of the forest's song,
Invites us to stay, to linger long,
Each step we take on mossy ground,
A deeper connection with life profound.

Squirrels dart and birds take flight,
In harmony, they share their light,
In every sound, in every sigh,
The sacred bond as time slips by.

So let us pause, let spirits rise,
Under the cool and endless skies,
For in this haven, hearts entwine,
In nature's heart, our souls align.

A Breath of Forest Air

In the forest, the air is sweet,
Tickled leaves beneath our feet,
With every breath, the world slows down,
In this silence, joy is found.

The pine and cedar scent the breeze,
As sunlight dances through the trees,
Among the roots, our spirits soar,
In nature's arms, we're rich with more.

Birdsong weaves through branches high,
A lullaby that soothes the sky,
Each rustling leaf, a tale to share,
A secret bond in forest air.

The hidden paths invite our roam,
With every step, we feel at home,
The whispers of the woods compel,
In this embrace, our hearts will dwell.

So take a breath, let worries fade,
In this green world, our souls are laid,
Among the trees, our spirits share,
The vital pulse of forest air.

Secrets of the Silent Grove

In silent groves where shadows creep,
The secrets of the earth we keep,
Whispers linger in the air,
Tales of life, beyond compare.

Ancient trees, their roots run deep,
Guardians of the dreams we seek,
With every branch, a history,
Written in their majesty.

Ferns unfurl in gentle grace,
In every nook, a hidden space,
The silence sings, a lovely tune,
A symphony beneath the moon.

In every breeze, in every glance,
Nature invites us to dance,
Among the shadows, secrets lie,
In the silent grove, time drifts by.

So pause awhile, let thoughts take flight,
With every breath, find pure delight,
For in this grove, where shadows dwell,
We uncover what words can't tell.

Dappled Light and Gentle Breezes

Dappled light on paths we roam,
The forest whispers, welcomes home,
As sunbeams kiss the leafy floor,
We find a peace we've known before.

With gentle breezes, secrets flow,
Among the trees, a soft hello,
Each sigh of wind, a tranquil song,
In nature's heart, where we belong.

The vibrant blooms in colors bright,
Invite us in, a pure delight,
As petals dance on every gust,
In this embrace, we place our trust.

The rustling branches, the softest sighs,
A haven where our spirit flies,
In every shadow and every ray,
A reminder that love finds a way.

So here we'll stay, in tranquil bliss,
Amid the woods, we surely miss,
Dappled light and gentle breeze,
In nature's arms, our souls at ease.

Respite Within the Sylvan Space

A whisper of leaves in the still air,
The gentle sway of branches above.
Nature's embrace, a tender care,
A refuge found, a peaceful love.

The sun peeks through, a golden glow,
Casting shadows on the forest floor.
In this haven, worries let go,
As silence opens a soothing door.

Birds take flight, a joyous display,
Their melodies float on the breeze.
In moments like this, time fades away,
Surrounded by trees, my spirit's ease.

Moss carpets ground, soft underfoot,
While brook's soft murmur sings to me.
I breathe in deep, my heart takes root,
In this sylvan space, I feel free.

With every breath, a world anew,
In the arms of nature, I find peace.
Respite here, a dream come true,
My soul and heart, at last, release.

Dappled Light and Quiet Thoughts

In the glen where shadows play,
Sunlight dances on the ground.
Each ray a spark, brightening the day,
In this moment, solace found.

Mossy stones, cool to the touch,
Underneath the branches' sweep.
Nature's lull, a soothing hush,
In the heart, a promise to keep.

Dappled light upon my face,
Whispers of the wind so sweet.
In this sacred, timeless space,
Each heartbeat slows, life feels complete.

Clouds drift by in a gentle race,
While worries fade like distant dreams.
Here, in this enchanted place,
The mind unwinds, or so it seems.

Thoughts like petals in a stream,
Floating softly, one by one.
In dappled light, I find my theme,
A quiet heart, where life's begun.

Enchanted by the Evergreen Horizon

Where pines reach high to touch the sky,
The world unfolds in shades of green.
Beneath their watchful gaze, I sigh,
The whisper of beauty, a tranquil scene.

Mountains cradle secrets old,
In their shadows, stories hide.
Each tale in whispers, gently told,
In every breeze, the past abides.

Wildflowers bloom, bright and bold,
Their colors dance, a painter's brush.
In this realm where wonders unfold,
The heart beats fast, in nature's hush.

Every path leads to delight,
In this paradise, moments last.
The horizon glows with fading light,
While stars awaken, casting fast.

With every step, I learn to roam,
To seek, to feel, to simply be.
Enchanted here, I find my home,
The evergreen horizon sets me free.

Reflection Under the Broad Boughs

Beneath the boughs, shadows stretch wide,
A canvas painted with hues of earth.
In this quiet, my thoughts confide,
To nature's peace, I find my worth.

Rippling waters beckon near,
Their surface mirrors the sky's embrace.
In the stillness, I lose my fear,
And find my place in nature's grace.

The rustle of leaves tells a tale,
Of all who wandered this tranquil way.
In their whispers, I feel the scale,
Of life's great journey, come what may.

Time pauses here, a sacred trust,
Each breath a gift, each moment bright.
In shadows deep, away from dust,
I hold the dawn, I greet the night.

Reflection blooms under the trees,
Where thoughts are woven in the air.
In nature's quilt, my heart finds ease,
Under broad boughs, I am laid bare.

Soul-Soothing Spaces in Nature

In valleys where soft whispers play,
The sunlight dances, bright and gay.
Among the flowers, peace takes flight,
A gentle breeze, a pure delight.

Rivers murmur songs of old,
Their crystal tales, a treasure to hold.
Each step upon the verdant ground,
An echo of joy, a love unbound.

Mountains rise with dignity high,
Beneath their gaze, the spirits sigh.
In moments shared with nature's grace,
We find our hearts, our sacred place.

The quiet rustle of the leaves,
In every breath, our soul believes.
As twilight drapes the world in gold,
We seek the stories yet untold.

In nature's arms, we find our way,
In her embrace, we long to stay.
Each moment paused, a snapshot rare,
Soul-soothing spaces, beyond compare.

Composure in the Woodland Shade

In woodland depths where shadows play,
A sanctuary from the fray.
Trees stretch out their mighty hands,
To cradle peace in quiet lands.

The softest whispers ride the breeze,
In harmony with rustling leaves.
A carpet rich with moss and pine,
Where every footstep feels divine.

Sunlight filters through the boughs,
Illuminating nature's vows.
Each sigh of wind, a soothing balm,
In quietude, our hearts are calm.

The scent of earth, the song of birds,
A tranquil space without the words.
We linger 'neath the verdant shade,
In nature's hush, our fears allayed.

Time slows down within this grove,
In every heartbeat, we feel loved.
Composure finds us, deep and wide,
In woodland's arms, we gently bide.

Under the Pine's Quiet Repose

Beneath the pines, where shadows blend,
The world doth pause, and troubles end.
A sanctuary for the mind,
In fragrant air, release we find.

Soft needles whisper stories old,
Each breath we take, a prayer unfold.
The gentle sway of branches high,
A lullaby that draws a sigh.

Amidst the bark, in twilight's glow,
We lay our burdens down and slow.
The spirit dances in the glade,
In pine's embrace, our fears afraid.

The heart beats steady, calm and true,
In nature's realm, we are renewed.
Under the pine's quiet repose,
We find the peace that softly grows.

A moment captured, still and bright,
In sacred hours before the night.
This hallowed ground, our souls embrace,
In pine's warm arms, we find our place.

Nature's Gentle Embrace

In golden fields where wildflowers sway,
Nature wraps us, come what may.
With open arms, she draws us near,
In every sigh, her love is clear.

The mountain streams with laughter flow,
Carving paths where dreams can grow.
Each pebble whispers tales untold,
Of ancient roots and spirits bold.

Underneath the sapphire skies,
The gentle breeze, a lullaby.
With every rustle, every sound,
In nature's heart, true peace is found.

The dusk that paints the world in hues,
A vibrant canvas, nature's muse.
We're cradled close, embraced with grace,
In nature's arms, we find our place.

As night descends, the stars appear,
A twinkling guide that calms our fear.
In every shadow, love interlace,
In nature's gentle, warm embrace.

A Healing Touch from Nature's Hand

In the whisper of the breeze, softly blown,
Gentle waves of green, a calming tone.
Each leaf a promise, the earth's sweet grace,
Nature's hand cradles, a warm embrace.

Sunlight dances on petals bright,
Every shadow reveals pure light.
Rivers murmur secrets, old and wise,
Hope is reborn, beneath clear skies.

Mountains stand tall, a sturdy friend,
In their presence, worries mend.
Footsteps lead to where the wild things thrive,
In nature's quilt, we feel alive.

Seasons shift, a gentle song,
Through every change, we still belong.
With every heartbeat, the forest sings,
A healing touch that nature brings.

Let the world fade, just for a while,
Find solace in nature, and smile.
For in her arms, we shed our woes,
In this silence, true peace grows.

Delicate Specks of Pine Dust

In the forest's heart, where shadows play,
Pine dust whispers of the day.
A sprinkle of dreams on soft, green beds,
Nature's secrets where the path treads.

Beneath tall trees that stretch and sway,
The scent of earth, a sweet ballet.
Delicate specks dance in the light,
Carried away, a wondrous sight.

Among the needles, life unfolds,
Stories of ages in whispers told.
Tiny creatures, in quiet bliss,
In every corner, a hidden kiss.

The wind carries tales from afar,
With every gust, we feel the star.
Pine dust lingers, a gentle haze,
In nature's world, we lose our gaze.

Moments fade like the sun's last glow,
In that stillness, our spirits grow.
Delicate pieces, life's gentle trust,
In the woods, we find our must.

So let the pine dust settle deep,
In our hearts, its magic keep.
For in its embrace, we find our sight,
Delicate specks, pure and light.

Dreams Weave in the Cool Shade

In the cool shade, where the moss lies thick,
Dreams weave softly, a gentle flick.
A tapestry woven with threads of green,
In nature's embrace, all is serene.

The brook sings low, a lullaby sweet,
As wishes take flight on whispering feet.
Clouds drift by, like thoughts set free,
In the world's hush, we just let be.

Every rustle brings stories anew,
In that stillness, we find the true.
Birds call softly, each note a line,
In the verses of nature, our hearts entwine.

Light filters down through branches high,
A golden touch as moments fly.
With every breath, we gather hope,
In this cool shade, we learn to cope.

It's here in the quiet, we pause in space,
As dreams find wings, they softly trace.
The magic of moments held so divine,
In the cool shade, our spirits shine.

So linger a while, let your mind roam,
In the tapestry of nature, we find home.
For among the trees, our dreams will stay,
Woven forever in nature's play.

Bound by the Roots of Stillness

In the silence deep, where the shadows breathe,
Bound by the roots that gently weave.
Each moment anchored in nature's embrace,
Time stands still in this sacred place.

The world fades away, a distant sound,
Here in the stillness, our hearts are found.
With every heartbeat, the earth aligns,
In roots of solace, our spirit shines.

Branches stretch wide, to cradle the sun,
In this grand tapestry, we are one.
Whispers of life in each rustling leaf,
Nature's caress, a shared belief.

Grounded like trees, our troubles cease,
In quiet strength, we find our peace.
The pulse of the earth, a guiding light,
In the roots of stillness, we take flight.

So pause for a moment, close your eyes,
In nature's heart, our spirit flies.
For in the calm, we're never alone,
Bound by the roots, we find our home.

With every breath, a connection grows,
In this stillness, our wisdom flows.
Together we flourish, together we heal,
Bound by the roots, our truth revealed.

Resting in Nature's Arms

Underneath the ancient trees,
Whispers float upon the breeze.
Gentle leaves and dappled light,
Cradling dreams in soft twilight.

Mossy beds where silence lies,
Nature's peace beneath the skies.
Birdsong sings a lullaby,
Soothing hearts as time drifts by.

Streams that giggle, rocks that smile,
Harmony that spans a mile.
In this haven, time stands still,
Nature's beauty, purest thrill.

Green Shadows and Soft Lullabies

In the glade where shadows dance,
Nature weaves a sweet romance.
Leaves that shimmer, softly sway,
Guiding thoughts that drift away.

Crickets chirp their evening song,
Echoes where the heart belongs.
Moonlight paints the world in gold,
Fables of the night unfold.

Gentle breezes weave their tales,
Carrying the scent of trails.
Wrapped in dreams beneath the trees,
Hearts find rest amidst the leaves.

A Stillness Wrapped in Green

Quiet woods with shadows deep,
Where the ancient secrets keep.
Every rustle, every sound,
Nature's calmness all around.

Sunbeams trickle through the boughs,
Painting patterns on the cows.
Butterflies in silent flight,
Dancing softly, pure delight.

Inhale the scent of earth and pine,
Feel the universe align.
Moments captured, time stands still,
In this green embrace, we will.

Secrets Within the Forest Veil

In the woods where shadows hide,
Mysteries of old abide.
Whispers ride the evening air,
Hints of magic everywhere.

Footsteps soft on carpeted ground,
Nature's heartbeat is the sound.
Every fern and winding vine,
Holds a story, pure and fine.

Hidden paths and glimmers bright,
Leading us to realms of light.
Hold the wonder, breathe it in,
Let the journey then begin.

Clusters of Calm in the Woods

Whispers soft beneath the leaves,
Gentle breezes weave and breathe.
Sunlight filters through the green,
Nature's peace, a tranquil scene.

Mossy carpets, paths before,
Footsteps hush, we seek for more.
Every shadow tells a tale,
In the woods where spirits sail.

Birdsong dances, sweet and clear,
Echoes lull, we're gathered near.
Clusters of calm, a sacred blend,
In the forest, time will bend.

Each moment stretches like a string,
Heartbeats slow, our spirits sing.
Lost in wonder, lost in bliss,
Nature's cradle, nothing amiss.

As stillness settles, eyes will close,
Dreams awaken, thoughts compose.
Under the canopy, we find,
Clusters of calm, heart and mind.

Pine-Scented Daydreams

Amidst the needles, whispers grow,
Breath of pine, a soft echo.
Daydreams linger, drift away,
Nature's charm, come out and play.

Golden rays through branches peep,
In this haven, silence deep.
Rustling leaves and distant calls,
Pine-scented air in tranquil halls.

Time unfolds in lazy streams,
Laughter dances, life redeems.
Clouds like cotton, drifting high,
In this moment, we could fly.

Starlit skies, the world awake,
Nature's canvas, hearts to take.
With every breath, we come alive,
Pine-scented dreams, we will thrive.

Memory lingers, scents entwined,
Every moment, sweetly designed.
Through the forest, we shall roam,
In daydreams' arms, we find our home.

Timelessness Beneath Ancient Trees

Beneath the reaches of old boughs,
Time stands still, a silent vow.
Roots entwined with earth's embrace,
History carves a sacred space.

Leaves that whisper tales of yore,
Echoes dance forevermore.
Hands of time in shadows cast,
In this haven, memories last.

Air imbued with ancient grace,
We find solace in this place.
Moments merge, a soft caress,
Timelessness in nature's dress.

Branches cradle dreams anew,
Underneath the sky so blue.
Here our worries fade away,
Beneath the trees, we choose to stay.

With each heartbeat, wisdom grows,
In nature's lap, true magic flows.
Timeless bonds in roots we bind,
Beneath the trees, our spirits find.

A Pause in the Heart of Nature

In the stillness, senses wake,
Nature pauses, hearts then take.
Breaths align with gentle winds,
In this moment, silence begins.

Leaves are dancing, shadows play,
Every worry drifts away.
Sunlight paints the world in gold,
A sacred space where dreams unfold.

Crickets sing as dusk descends,
Nature's peace, where time suspends.
With open hearts, we will receive,
In this pause, we shall believe.

Birds return to nests at night,
Fading echoes, soft twilight.
In the heart of woods so vast,
A pause hidden in the past.

Nature whispers, we should linger,
Softly beckoning with a finger.
In her arms, we rest and sigh,
A pause in nature, dreams can fly.

Moments of Maple and Fir

In the glade where shadows play,
Maple leaves dance, bright and gay.
A whispering breeze sings through the boughs,
Time slows down, it takes a pause.

The fir stands strong, a sentinel true,
Guarding secrets of the dew.
Sunlight filters, a golden hue,
Moments cherished, ever new.

Crimson and gold in autumn's embrace,
Nature's canvas, a timeless grace.
Each leaf falls, a story untold,
Life's fleeting, yet never old.

When winter comes with its frosty breath,
The world dons a coat, a quiet death.
But beneath the snow, life waits in peace,
In nature's heart, all sorrows cease.

Spring blooms forth, a vibrant sigh,
With each new bud, the past slips by.
Maple and fir, a bond divine,
In moments shared, our hearts align.

Sanctuary of the Stalwart Pines

In a grove of towering might,
Pines stand guard with edges bright.
Whispered hymns in rustling leaves,
A sanctuary where the spirit breathes.

Soft shadows cloak the forest floor,
Each step taken opens a door.
To memories held in branches wide,
A refuge where the heart can bide.

Through the seasons, they remain,
Standing firm through sun and rain.
Roots entwined beneath the ground,
In their embrace, peace is found.

Creatures wander, the forest's kin,
Sharing tales of where they've been.
Underneath the canopy's grace,
Find solace, a tranquil space.

The moonlight pours through gaps above,
Guiding dreams like whispers of love.
In the solemn hush of night,
The pines watch over, holding tight.

Harmony in the Heartwood

Deep within the ancient trees,
Harmony flows on the gentle breeze.
Whispered secrets from olden days,
In the heartwood, nature's praise.

Branches sway, a symphony played,
Composing light in the forest's shade.
Birds take flight, a graceful arc,
In unity, they dance till dark.

Moss carpets ground, soft and green,
Rich earth alive with the unseen.
Roots intertwine, a network wide,
Holding stories, a timeless guide.

As daylight wanes and stars appear,
The heartwood hums, so sweet and clear.
In the space where silence reigns,
All is one, where love remains.

Together, we find our place,
In the forest's warm embrace.
For in the heartwood, we belong,
A chorus sung, a timeless song.

Beneath the Shield of Green

Underneath the leafy crown,
Where sunlight drips and shadows drown.
Nature's breath, a cooling balm,
In the stillness, the world is calm.

A hoot rings out from distant trees,
Echoing through the gentle breeze.
Life abounds in hidden sights,
Underneath the starry nights.

Cascading streams weave tales of old,
Glittering silver and threads of gold.
With every ripple, a story flows,
In the quiet, peace only grows.

Beneath the shield where green does sway,
The tapestry of life holds sway.
In harmony with all that's seen,
We find our place, beneath the green.

Forever intertwined, we thrive,
In nature's heart, we come alive.
A sanctuary where dreams seem clear,
Beneath the shield, we hold so dear.

Soft Murmurs of Foliage

Whispers dance on gentle breeze,
Leaves entwined in secret pleas.
Sunlight weaves a golden thread,
Nature's song where footsteps tread.

Rustling tales from branch to ground,
Softly in the air they sound.
Patterns cast in light and shade,
In this peace, my heart is made.

Petals fall in silent grace,
Time held still in this embraced space.
Every shade a story spun,
In the hush, all worries done.

Tangles of green, a soft cocoon,
Crickets sing beneath the moon.
Quiet moments linger long,
Where the soul finds its own song.

In the dappled light I find,
Echoes of a wandering mind.
Nature's calm, a gentle balm,
In these woods, my heart is warm.

Perspectives Under the Verdant Roof

Underneath this leafy dome,
I discover my quiet home.
Every branch holds stories deep,
Each soft shadow, secrets keep.

Up above, the sunlight plays,
Crafting patterns in bright rays.
Flickering from leaf to ground,
In this haven, peace is found.

Eyes closed tight, I breathe it in,
As the forest hums within.
An awakening of the soul,
Here, I feel completely whole.

Rustling leaves, a nature's choir,
Notes of life, they never tire.
With each step, a new delight,
Guided gently by soft light.

A tapestry of greens and golds,
Each journey's art, a story told.
In the calm, I see anew,
The world beneath this verdant hue.

Ferns and Fables of the Wooded Realm

In a glade where ferns unfold,
Every shadow, a tale retold.
Mossy carpets, rich and green,
Secrets nestled, seldom seen.

With each step, the stories wake,
Whispers of the path I take.
Leaves converse in muted tones,
Echoing the earth's soft groans.

Moonlit nights and sunlit days,
Sketch the forest's endless ways.
In the hush, I hear the past,
Fables spun, forever vast.

Rustling secrets, all around,
Magic woven in the ground.
In this realm of ancient trees,
Heart and mind are set at ease.

Dreams awaken, wild and free,
Here, in nature's tapestry.
Ferns and fables intertwine,
In these woods, my spirit shines.

Soil and Stillness in the Shade

Beneath the canopy of green,
Life lies hidden, never seen.
Soil and stillness softly blend,
Creating space where troubles end.

Roots stretch wide, anchoring deep,
Softly cradling all that sleep.
In the shade, my thoughts unwind,
Nature's peace, a treasure find.

Every rustle stirs the air,
Calling forth a silent prayer.
Gentle breezes brush my skin,
In this calm, I breathe within.

Colors mingle, scents arise,
In this stillness, calm complies.
Here, I sit, a moment's grace,
Life embraced in nature's space.

With the soil, I weave my fate,
In this shade, the world is great.
Serenity, a gift so rare,
In the stillness, I lay bare.

Resting in Resilient Heights

In the embrace of mountains high,
Where the eagles soar and the shadows lie,
Whispers of strength ride the breeze,
Nature's rhythm puts the heart at ease.

Among the stones and ancient trees,
A sanctuary where the spirit flees,
Roots gripping earth, steadfast, and bold,
Stories of the ages quietly unfold.

Sunset paints with fiery hues,
A canvas where the heart renews,
In every breath, a tranquil hymn,
Resting here, the worries dim.

Stars emerge in the velvet night,
Guiding souls with twinkling light,
Each moment spent among the heights,
Offer solace, wondrous sights.

In resilient realms, we find our place,
A bond with nature, a gentle grace,
So let the world fade far away,
In these heights, we long to stay.

Stillness Amongst the Conifers

Whispers echo in the forest deep,
Among the conifers, secrets keep,
Gentle rustling, a soft embrace,
Nature's cradle, a sacred space.

Moss carpets ground, a lush green bed,
Underfoot, where all fears are shed,
Sunlight dances through needle's lace,
Illuminating this tranquil place.

With every breath, the stillness grows,
In the silence, the spirit knows,
Each tree stands with stories to tell,
Of time's passage and nature's spell.

Here, the heart learns to unwind,
In the peace of the forest, we find,
A harmony that soothes the soul,
Amongst the conifers, we feel whole.

As twilight falls, shadows extend,
In this stillness, we begin to mend,
Nature's symphony sings sweet and clear,
In these woods, we lose our fear.

Nature's Velvet Embrace

Softly cradled in nature's arms,
Wrapped in beauty, the world disarms,
Petals whisper secrets in the breeze,
The heart finds comfort, calm, and peace.

Meadows bloom in hues divine,
Where honey bees and butterflies twine,
Golden sunlight bathes each petal,
Nature's tapestry begins to settle.

A stream gurgles its gentle song,
Inviting spirits to linger long,
Over rocks, under boughs it flows,
In every ripple, patience grows.

As day lays down its vibrant hues,
The sky transforms, a canvas renewed,
Stars emerge like silken threads,
Weaving dreams where the heart treads.

In nature's arms, we find our grace,
A velvet embrace, a sacred space,
As the world spins in a frenzied race,
We find solace in this embrace.

A Refuge in the Rustic Green

Nestled deep in a woodland scene,
There lies a refuge, a rustic green,
Where the past meets the present's grace,
In every leaf, a familiar face.

Stone pathways wind through mossy beds,
Nature's fingers where sunlight spreads,
Tall oaks stand like sentinels proud,
Whispering stories, quiet yet loud.

The air is filled with sweet decay,
Life and death in a graceful ballet,
Crickets chirp their evening song,
In this sanctuary, we belong.

As twilight wraps the world in gold,
The tales of the forest are softly told,
In rustic views, our hearts align,
Breathing in peace, we intertwine.

Here, we shelter, away from haste,
In nature's arms, we find our place,
A refuge in green, forever stand,
Connected to earth, hand in hand.

Whispers of the Forest Floor

Gentle winds weave through the leaves,
Softly cradling secrets old.
Beneath the roots, the earth believes,
In stories waiting to be told.

Mossy beds where sunlight gleams,
A carpet green, a tender blush.
Nature's quilt of whispered dreams,
Awakes the world in twilight hush.

Tiny creatures scurry near,
Their laughter echoes in the glade.
Each footstep, all that's left unclear,
Amidst the beauty, they parade.

Fingers trace the ancient bark,
Timeworn tales in every line.
Within the forest's sacred arc,
The past and present intertwine.

In every shadow, every sigh,
The forest breathes, a living lore.
Beneath a vast and watchful sky,
The whispers linger evermore.

Shadows of Silent Trees

The trees stand tall, their branches sway,
    Casting shadows on the ground.
In twilight's glow, they softly play,
    With secrets not yet found.

Each whisper through the timbered heights,
    Hints at tales of ages past.
In moonlit nights, their whispers ignite,
    While stillness holds them fast.

Mysterious forms with stories worn,
    Guardians of the ancient land.
In their embrace, we're reborn,
    Connected by a gentle hand.

As night falls deep and stars emerge,
    The roots entangle, strong and deep.
In nature's heart, a quiet surge,
    Of life and dreams that softly seep.

The forest breathes, a sacred space,
    Where shadows dance and spirits roam.
In every corner, time and place,
    Whisper us back to our home.

In the Embrace of Evergreen

Where evergreens stand proud and strong,
A fortress green against the sky.
In their embrace, we belong,
As time drifts gently by.

The scent of pine fills up the air,
A balm for hearts that seek to heal.
In nature's cradle, free of care,
We find the peace that feels so real.

Branches sway in a tender dance,
Their needle tips a soothing kiss.
In every sway, a fleeting chance,
To lose ourselves in nature's bliss.

Above us, whispers of the breeze,
Carried on the wings of dreams.
Beneath the boughs, our spirits ease,
As daylight fades and starlight beams.

In the embrace of evergreen,
Our worries fade like morning mist.
In this quiet space, serene,
Life's beautiful moments persist.

Serenity in the Canopy

In the canopy, light filters through,
A tapestry spun of green and gold.
A tranquil world, a dream anew,
In the stories of life retold.

Each leaf dances in the gentle breeze,
A soft enchantment, sweet and rare.
Nature hums its quiet pleas,
In this sanctuary we share.

The birds compose a melody,
While sunlight paints the dappled ground.
In the soft embrace of calm, we see,
A universe in silence found.

Murmurs flow from hidden streams,
Nestled beneath the leafy dome.
In the heart of nature's dreams,
We find a place that feels like home.

As twilight drapes its velvet cloak,
Stars thread through the fabric of night.
In the quiet, our spirits soak,
In serenity, pure and bright.

The Poetry of Pine Cones Falling

Beneath the trees, a gentle sigh,
Pine cones tumble from sky to ground.
Each soft thud, a whispered goodbye,
Nature's rhythm, a soothing sound.

Cradled by earth, they find their home,
In the forest's embrace, they rest.
Silent witnesses, they silently roam,
In nature's cradle, forever blessed.

Frosted mornings cloak the wood,
Candles of warmth in winter's chill.
They scatter seeds for futurehood,
Promising life, a timeless thrill.

With every fall, a story told,
Of seasons changing, winds that call.
In every pin, a trace of old,
The dance of nature, never small.

So let us pause, and heed the fall,
Of pine cones tender, soft, and round.
In tiny whispers, nature's thrall,
Reminds us all of beauty found.

Nature's Embrace in the Breezy Hollow

In the hollow where soft winds play,
Trees sway gently, leaves converse.
Sunlight filters through the fray,
Nature's cradle, the universe.

A whispering brook sings sweet and clear,
Caressing stones with gentle grace.
In this refuge, there's naught to fear,
Embraced by nature's warm embrace.

Wildflowers bloom in bursts of hue,
Calling to bees and butterflies.
Each petal glistens, fresh as dew,
A painted canvas beneath the skies.

Mountains guard this sacred space,
A sentinel of rock and time.
In their shadows, we find our place,
Where nature's heartbeat feels sublime.

As daylight fades, the stars ignite,
Painting dreams where shadows weave.
In nature's arms, we find our light,
A sanctuary, forever to believe.

The Sound of Silence in the Spellbound Pines

In spellbound pines, the silence hums,
A melody of stillness deep.
Among the boughs, the heartbeat drums,
Where ancient secrets wait and sleep.

Soft needles carpet the forest floor,
Where footsteps echo, yet scarcely sound.
In quietude, we yearn for more,
In whispers lost, where dreams are found.

Misty mornings cloak the trees,
Veiling shadows in a soft embrace.
A tranquil dance upon the breeze,
Resonating in this sacred space.

Each sigh of wind tells tales untold,
Of forgotten days and fleeting time.
In this stillness, the heart unfolds,
Embracing nature's silent rhyme.

The moonlight bathes the pines in glow,
Guardians of secrets, wise and true.
In spellbound silence, we come to know,
The sound of nature calls to you.

Dreamscapes of Green and Gold

In dreamscapes vast where green unfolds,
Golden rays weave through the trees.
A tapestry of stories told,
In whispers carried by the breeze.

Every leaf a memory bright,
Dancing softly, swaying light.
Nature beckons with pure delight,
In these dreamscapes, hearts take flight.

The winding paths of moss and stone,
Lead us deeper into the wild.
In every step, we're not alone,
Embracing beauty, nature's child.

The call of birds sings high above,
A symphony of life and grace.
Wrapped in warmth, like hands of love,
In nature's heart, we find our place.

As twilight casts its golden hue,
A canvas painted just for us.
In dreamscapes where the wild things grew,
We find our solace, free of fuss.

Forest Reveries

In the hush of green, I tread,
Whispers of trees above my head.
Soft moss cushions every step,
Nature's secrets, quietly kept.

Sunbeams filter through the leaves,
Dancing light as the forest breathes.
Birdsong weaves a gentle tune,
Heartbeats sync with the afternoon.

Amidst ferns and wildflowers fair,
Magic twirls in fragrant air.
Every path leads to a dream,
Crafted in nature's flowing stream.

Beneath, the earth is rich and deep,
In silent shadows, secrets sleep.
Here I find my spirit's call,
In the woodland's embrace, I fall.

A symphony of leaves and skies,
Nature's wonders hypnotize.
Lost in these forest reveries,
I breathe in peace, I feel the trees.

Nature's Peace

Gentle whispers on the breeze,
Nature's calm brings heart to ease.
Every sigh, a soft caress,
In the wild, we feel our best.

Mountains rise with silent grace,
Holding time in their embrace.
Rivers flow with tranquil song,
In their presence, we belong.

Wildflowers bloom in colors bright,
Painting meadows, a pure delight.
Beneath the sky, vast and wide,
Nature's peace, our hearts are tied.

Clouds drift lazily on high,
Like dreams floating in the sky.
Stars emerge when day is done,
In the night, our souls are one.

Nature's pulse, a steady beat,
Guides us gently, oh so sweet.
In this world, we find our place,
Wrapped in nature's warm embrace.

Underneath the Skyward Giants

Towering trees touch the sky,
Whispering secrets with every sigh.
Roots deep within the earth's embrace,
Time stands still in this sacred space.

Leaves rustle in a gentle dance,
Inviting me to take a chance.
Sunlight dapples the forest floor,
An open invitation to explore.

Nests cradle life in branches broad,
Each tiny chirp a sweet applaud.
Underneath the skyward giants,
Life unfolds in bright defiance.

Shadows play beneath the boughs,
Nature bows, and peace allows.
With every breath, I feel the earth,
In quiet awe, I find my worth.

Time drifts softly like the leaves,
In nature's arms, my spirit believes.
Underneath the skyward giants,
I find solace, my heart defiant.

Reverent Rest in the Forest's Heart

In the heart where silence reigns,
Peace envelops, calms my pains.
Golden light through branches streams,
Here, I rest within my dreams.

Murmuring brooks in radiant flow,
Secrets of the earth in tow.
Ferns unfurl with graceful ease,
Nature offers hope and peace.

Squirrels chatter, birds take flight,
Life awakens in soft light.
In stillness, I find my way,
Guided by the light of day.

Roots entwine beneath my feet,
Life's foundation feels complete.
In the forest, time stands still,
Cradled by the ancient will.

Moments drift like drifting leaves,
In nature's heart, the spirit breathes.
Reverent rest, a life anew,
In the woods, I find my view.

Shadows That Dance in the Breeze

Softly sway the shadows low,
In the forest, where secrets grow.
Breezes play a wild refrain,
As light and dark entwine again.

Murmurs of the leaves above,
Nature breathes with gentle love.
Sunshine spills on golden ground,
In this haven, joy is found.

The dance of shadows paints the day,
In playful hues, the world at play.
Rustling whispers call to me,
In this realm of purest glee.

Dappled patterns softly shift,
Nature's art, a precious gift.
Every moment etched in light,
A tapestry of day and night.

As evening falls, the stars will glance,
Illuminating shadows' dance.
In the woods, my heart takes flight,
In the calm of fading light.

Respite in the Woodland Whisper

In the shade where shadows play,
Gentle breezes drift and sway.
Leaves like whispers in the air,
Nature's peace is everywhere.

Mossy beds where silence sings,
Comfort found in simple things.
Woodland paths that softly wind,
A secret solace we're to find.

Sunlight dances on the ground,
In this grove, new joys abound.
Birds call out, the world awakes,
Each moment sweet, no heartache makes.

Time stands still; we simply breathe,
In this haven, we believe.
Nature's arms stretch wide and free,
Here, we find tranquility.

So we linger, hearts at ease,
In this woodland, feel the peace.
Respite found in every leaf,
Nature's touch, a soft relief.

Cool Nooks of Nature's Embrace

Beneath the boughs, in shadows deep,
Cool nooks whisper secrets keep.
Rivulets that softly murmur,
Nature's heart, a gentle fervor.

In the glade where wildflowers bloom,
Colors dance and scents consume.
Every petal holds a dream,
In the sunlight's golden beam.

Moss and stone, a resting place,
Where time and worries lose their race.
Through the ferns, the echoes play,
A symphony of green ballet.

Bees hum soft, a lullaby,
While the clouds drift in the sky.
In these cool nooks, we immerse,
Nature speaks, the universe.

Freedom found in every sigh,
With the wind, we learn to fly.
These cool nooks, our sacred space,
Cradle us in nature's grace.

Elegy for the Evergreen Space

In the shade where giants stand,
Whispers weave through verdant land.
Time-travel in a moment's glance,
Nature's timeless, haunting dance.

Silent sentinel trees keep guard,
Holding tales of times so hard.
Each ring a story carved in years,
Beneath their weight, the heart just fears.

Boughs that shelter, roots that grip,
Secrets lay in nature's script.
An elegy for breaths long past,
Echoes of a silence vast.

Yet in their shade, life springs anew,
Green shoots break ground, the morning dew.
This cycle spins, both loss and gain,
In every joy, there is a pain.

With heavy hearts, we say goodbye,
To the whispers, our spirits fly.
In this evergreen space we mourn,
But in its grace, we are reborn.

Gentle Rest Among the Giants

Beneath the arms of ancient trees,
A gentle rest wrapped in the breeze.
Roots that twist like stories told,
Hearts find solace, warm and bold.

Long shadows stretch across the ground,
In stillness, deeper peace is found.
Leaves above like whispers sway,
Time is lost; we choose to stay.

Sunlight filters through the green,
A tapestry of calm unseen.
With every breath, the world slows down,
Here, we exchange our busy crown.

Among the giants, we align,
In shared silence, hearts entwine.
Each moment savored, softly blessed,
Finding comfort, gentle rest.

So let us linger in this space,
Tracing time's unhurried grace.
Among the giants, we reside,
Nature's arms, our faithful guide.

The Language of Leafy Breezes

Whispers of green in the air,
Dancing leaves with secrets to share.
Waves of laughter in rustling sound,
Nature speaks where peace is found.

Sunlight filters through the trees,
Gentle caresses, a cool, soft breeze.
Branches sway in a rhythmic sway,
Telling stories of each passing day.

A symphony sung by wings that glide,
Songs of joy where dreams reside.
In nature's choir, every tone,
Leaves in harmony, never alone.

Colors blend in a painter's brush,
Emerald hues that softly brush.
Each fluttering leaf, a vibrant tale,
In the hush of woods, in the calm gale.

Beneath the canopy, life's embrace,
Time stands still in this sacred space.
The language spoken in every breeze,
Whispers the heart, and brings us peace.

A Retreat of Softness and Green

In a grove where shadows play,
A tranquil realm, a soft ballet.
Mossy carpets, cool and deep,
Nature cradles, lulling to sleep.

Velvet ferns and blooming flowers,
Time forgotten in these hours.
Sunlight dapples on the ground,
With peace, our souls are tightly wound.

The rustling trees, a calming sigh,
Here the heart learns to fly.
Butterflies dancing in the light,
A sweet escape, pure delight.

With every breath, we find our peace,
Letting go as tensions cease.
In this retreat, our spirits gleam,
Wrapped in nature's gentle dream.

Soft whispers of the winds around,
In this haven, joy is found.
A sanctuary, lush and serene,
A retreat of softness and green.

Embraced by the Piney Tranquility

In the arms of pines, we sigh,
Waves of calm as moments fly.
Needles whisper in the breeze,
Cradling hearts beneath the trees.

Scented air, a soothing balm,
In the stillness, we find calm.
Underneath this emerald shade,
Time drifts softly, unafraid.

Birds sing secret melodies,
Echoing through the sturdy trees.
In this peace, we are renewed,
In nature's heart, forever glued.

Roots entwined in the fertile ground,
In the woods, our dreams are found.
Embraced by the pines, we belong,
In the quiet, we grow strong.

Each step leads to a sacred space,
Where love and nature interlace.
In tranquil pines, we come alive,
Embraced by the calm, we thrive.

Solitude's Nest in the Pines

High above, the branches sway,
In solitude, we find our way.
Pinecones scatter on the floor,
Whispers of past lives, evermore.

Underneath a vast blue sky,
Birds in freedom, soaring high.
Nature's song, a soft embrace,
In this nest, we find our place.

With every rustle, secrets bloom,
A world ignited in nature's womb.
Silence wraps us, warm and tight,
In solitude, we ignite the light.

Memory lingers in the air,
In each moment, we lay bare.
Here within the swaying pine,
Solitude's nest, our spirits align.

The heartbeats dance with the breeze,
Finding solace, bringing ease.
In the pines, we heal and grow,
In solitude's nest, our spirits flow.

Cool Breezes and Sunlit Dreams

The morning sun peeks through the trees,
Gentle whispers carried on the breeze.
Golden rays dance on the grassy ground,
In this moment, peace is found.

Butterflies flutter in the warm sun's light,
Colors swirling in a joyful flight.
Each breath a treasure, so fresh and clear,
Filling hearts with joy, far and near.

Clouds drift lazily, like thoughts in the mind,
Worries fade with the ties that bind.
In the distance, laughter rings out loud,
From a child chasing dreams, feeling proud.

Evening skies transform with a hue,
Painting horizons in shades of blue.
Cool breezes whisper secrets of night,
Cradling dreams until morning light.

In the twilight, stars begin to gleam,
Guiding wanderers through the soft stream.
A world of wonder awaits to explore,
Cool breezes and dreams forevermore.

Beneath the Guardian Branches

Underneath the branches wide,
Nature offers a place to hide.
Whispers of leaves in a gentle dance,
Invite the soul to take a chance.

Sunbeams filter through the green,
Creating a world, serene and clean.
Birds sing sweetly in a joyful choir,
Fueling hearts with their warm desire.

Moss cushions softly beneath the feet,
Where peace and solitude meet.
A tranquil haven, a sacred space,
Guarded by nature's warm embrace.

Clouds drift slowly in the azure sky,
While time escapes, and moments fly.
Each heartbeat echoes the song of life,
In the stillness, free from strife.

As shadows lengthen and daylight fades,
The forest glows with lucent shades.
Beneath these branches, dreams take flight,
In the embrace of the coming night.

Tranquil Moments in the Woods

In the woods where silence sings,
Nature wraps her gentle wings.
Softly padding on the ground,
Peace in every glimpse around.

Sunlight dapples through the trees,
Kissing petals in the breeze.
Murmuring streams with crystal flow,
Whisper secrets only they know.

Ferns unfurl in shades of green,
A vibrant life, a hidden scene.
Shade and light blend as they play,
In this realm where dreams sway.

Each step forward, a moment to pause,
To witness nature's quiet applause.
Inhale deeply, let worries cease,
Find in the woods a timeless peace.

As daylight wanes and stars appear,
The nightingale sings sweet and clear.
Tranquil moments, forever adored,
In this sanctuary, the spirit soared.

A Symphony of Pine Needles

In a forest where the tall pines sway,
Nature's orchestra begins to play.
Melodies of rustling in the wind,
A symphony where dreams rescind.

Whispers rise with the morning dew,
Chiming softly, a song so true.
Pine cones scatter on the forest floor,
Inviting footsteps to explore more.

Sunlight filters through the evergreen,
Casting shadows on a vibrant scene.
A gentle hush blankets the night,
In the woods, every note feels right.

Crickets join as twilight calls,
Music echoes through ancient halls.
Nature's heartbeat, strong and pure,
In this symphony, we feel secure.

As night unfolds its velvet cloak,
Fireside stories, softly spoke.
Under starlit skies we find our place,
In harmony, we share this space.

Dreaming Under the Needled Roof

Beneath the pine, where whispers dwell,
A quiet world begins to swell.
Moonlit patches, shadows sway,
In dreams we weave, the night holds sway.

Stars above, like lanterns bright,
Guide our thoughts through velvet night.
In the hush, our spirits roam,
Finding peace, the heart's true home.

Gentle breezes, secrets shared,
Nature's grace, we feel prepared.
Wrapped in the warmth of soft embrace,
In this moment, we find grace.

With every breath, the stillness deep,
In this haven, we gently sleep.
Needled roof, a cozy dome,
In your calm, we've found our home.

Through the hours, time slips away,
In dreams beneath the needles' play.
Awake, asleep, where thoughts entwine,
Forever yours, this heart of mine.

Hushed Lullabies of the Pinewood

In the night, the trees softly sing,
Harmonies sweet in the cool spring.
Each note carries through the air,
A gentle touch, a soothing care.

Crickets chirp in rhythmic plight,
Adding music to the night.
Underneath the sky so wide,
Lullabies in which we hide.

Branches sway in tender grace,
In this moment, we find our place.
Nature's voice, a calming tide,
In your arms, I will abide.

Every breath a melody,
Serenading you and me.
Close your eyes, let worries cease,
In this lull, we find our peace.

At dawn's light, the song will change,
Yet our hearts will not estrange.
Hushed lullabies, forever keep,
Our dreams beneath the trees so deep.

Silence in the Shadowed Glade

In the glade where shadows play,
Silence reigns, it holds the sway.
Mossy carpets, tranquil sounds,
In this peace, our spirit grounds.

Dappled light waltzes through leaves,
Whispered secrets that nature weaves.
Beneath the boughs, we pause and take,
A breath within the calm we make.

Every rustle, soft embrace,
In the stillness, we find grace.
Echoes of the world outside,
Fading softly, like the tide.

Still the mind, let heartbeats hum,
In this sanctuary, we become.
Lost in wonder, time stands still,
Nature's heartbeat, a soothing thrill.

As twilight drapes its gentle shawl,
The quiet sings its silent call.
In the glade, forever laid,
Memories made, beneath the shade.

Under the Watchful Branches

Under branches stretched and wide,
Nature's wonders, we confide.
Each leaf whispers, a tale untold,
In their presence, we feel bold.

Gentle shadows dance with light,
Setting dreams upon our sight.
In this haven, burdens fade,
Underneath the leafy shade.

Birds above sing sweet and clear,
Melodies only we can hear.
Every note a soft caress,
In this moment, feel the bless.

Time it slows in this embrace,
Infinite, a sacred space.
With each breath, we intertwine,
Hearts united, yours and mine.

As the day turns into dusk,
In this place, we find our trust.
Under the branches, love shall grow,
In its warmth, forever glow.

Soft Shadows on the Ground

Beneath the trees, the whispers sigh,
Soft shadows dance as breezes fly.
Leaves flutter down like gentle rain,
Nature's embrace, a soothing refrain.

Footsteps linger on the path,
In the cool, the heart finds a bath.
Murmurs of life in twilight's glow,
A quiet rhythm, steady and slow.

Sunlight weaves through branches wide,
Painting stories where secrets hide.
In every corner, a tale awaits,
As dusk unveils the night's soft gates.

A world transformed in golden light,
Soft shadows cradle the creeping night.
Echoes of day, in silence they drown,
In a tapestry, deep and profound.

As stars awaken, dreams take flight,
Under the watch of the silver light.
In every flicker, hope is found,
In the soft shadows on the ground.

A Nest of Quietude

In branches high, a cradle sways,
Whispers echo through sunlit days.
Feathers soft, a lullaby sings,
Nestled close, the calmness brings.

A hidden world, serene and sweet,
Time slows down with every heartbeat.
The sky pours down a gentle hue,
As dreams unfold in morning dew.

With every breeze, a promise swells,
In the nest where silence dwells.
Crickets croon to the stars above,
In the hush of night, all is love.

Through soft branches, moonbeams play,
Lighting pathways where shadows lay.
A gentle peace wraps 'round the soul,
In a nest of quietude, we are whole.

Rejuvenation Under the Canopy

Beneath the boughs, life breathes anew,
Dappled light on the emerald hue.
Whispers of leaves, a symphony clear,
In the heart of the woods, joy draws near.

Roots stretch deep in the earth's embrace,
Finding strength in the gentle space.
Branches reaching for stars up high,
As the canopy sways, our spirits fly.

Mornings greet with a vibrant song,
Inviting us where we belong.
Nature's arms open wide and free,
In rejuvenation, we find the key.

As twilight beckons with dusk's soft sigh,
We gather dreams beneath the sky.
Life and love in perfect sync,
Under the canopy, we take a drink.

Every heartbeat, a rhythmic dance,
Under the trees, we take a chance.
In this haven, forever to stay,
Rejuvenation leads the way.

Pine-scented Reflections

Among the pines, the air is sweet,
Each step we take, a quiet beat.
Branches sway with stories untold,
Whispers of ages young and old.

The ground is soft beneath our feet,
Nature's chorus, a calming greet.
Scent of pine fills the open air,
In every moment, we find care.

Reflections dance on waters still,
As hearts unite with nature's will.
In the cool shade, we pause and breathe,
Here in the woods, we find reprieve.

Sunlight trickles through needles fine,
Guiding us home where hearts entwine.
Every rustle, a song we trace,
In pine-scented reflections, we find grace.

Memories linger in the gentle breeze,
Among the pines, we find our ease.
In this sacred place, we belong,
Pine-scented reflections, our heart's song.

Reverent Calm Among the Pines

In the stillness, shadows play,
Whispers of the winding way.
Sunlight dances through the leaves,
Where peace blooms and nature weaves.

Tall trunks embrace the sky's vast dome,
Branches cradle a heart, a home.
Mossy carpets tell silent stories,
Of ancient secrets and past glories.

A soft hush envelops the ground,
In this haven, solace is found.
Swaying ferns and distant calls,
Nature's warm embrace enthralls.

Gentle rustles of feathered wings,
Echo the joy that nature brings.
Within the pines, time stands still,
Awash in the woods, a sacred thrill.

Swaying with the Gentle Breezes

Whispers ride on the softest wind,
Through petals where the light has thinned.
Leaves sway in a graceful dance,
Nature's rhythm, a sweet romance.

Beneath the oak, where shadows lie,
Sunbeams filter through a sigh.
Grass sways softly, a verdant sea,
Encircling all in harmony.

With every gust, the world feels light,
A melody carried into the night.
In this embrace of earth and sky,
Life unfolds, as dreams drift by.

Dancing daisies in the glade,
Breezes weave through every shade.
Moments linger, time flows free,
Swaying gently, wild and free.

Starlit Evenings Among the Trees

As daylight fades to twilight's glow,
Stars awaken, one by one, they show.
Moonlight bathes the forest floor,
In the night, whispers softly soar.

Branches stretch to greet the sky,
An endless canvas where dreams fly.
Crickets sing their evening tune,
Beneath the watchful gaze of the moon.

In this hush, the heart finds peace,
Moments of magic never cease.
A tapestry of dreams unfold,
In silence, the stars tell stories old.

Twinkling gems in the velvet night,
Guiding wanderers with soft light.
Among the trees, a sacred space,
In starlit evenings, we embrace.

Harmony in Nature's Quietude

In the stillness, life resounds,
Nature's voice in whispers found.
Streams hum softly, a gentle song,
Where every element belongs.

Mountains stand with solemn grace,
Holding secrets in their embrace.
Birds call out, their joy declared,
In harmony, the wild is shared.

Blossoms sway with fragrant delight,
Colors dance in morning light.
The earth breathes in a tranquil sigh,
Underneath the vast, blue sky.

With every leaf that flutters down,
Nature wears her vibrant crown.
In quietude, where we reside,
Harmony and peace abide.

Whispers of the Woodland Shade

In the hush of the leaves, secrets flow,
Soft breezes sing, as shadows grow.
Moss carpets the ground, so gentle and green,
Nature's whispers echo, calm and serene.

Birds flit above, in their playful dance,
Sunbeams peek through, as if in a trance.
Each rustle and chirp tells stories untold,
In the woodland shade, a magic unfolds.

Roots intertwine, wrapping earth in a hug,
Life thrives below, in a snug little shrug.
With every soft sigh, the forest gives breath,
Whispers in twilight, a dance with sweet death.

Murmurs of streams, their melody flows,
Rippling softly where the wildflower grows.
Echoes of laughter from faraway streams,
In the woodland shade, we cradle our dreams.

We wander through paths where time loses track,
In nature's embrace, there's no need to look back.
Every heartbeat aligns with the land,
In whispers of shade, together we stand.

Tranquil Moments in Tall Trees

Among ancient trunks, stillness abides,
In the quiet embrace, where the spirit resides.
Golden rays filter, painting the ground,
In tranquil moments, a peace can be found.

Leaves rustle softly, in sweet harmony,
Whispers of nature, a soothing decree.
The world fades away, in this serene place,
Tranquility dwells, wrapped in nature's grace.

Branches stretch high, embracing the skies,
A sanctuary whispers where heartache defies.
In the arms of tall trees, we listen and heal,
In tranquil moments, our souls gently feel.

Crickets sing softly, as twilight descends,
The beauty of dusk as the day gently bends.
Here in this haven, all burdens unwind,
In moments of calm, true solace we find.

With each breath we take, the forest speaks true,
In its tranquil moments, we become renewed.
Together we stand, in unity's light,
In tall trees we gather, hearts open and bright.

Serenity in the Forest Canopy

High above ground, where the eagles do soar,
A quilt of green leaves, nature's vast floor.
Sunlight streams down through a lattice of leaves,
In the forest canopy, serenity weaves.

Gentle whispers float, like stories once lost,
In the arms of the trees, we count not the cost.
Every breeze carries peace, a healing embrace,
In the forest canopy, we find our true place.

Flickers of life in the shadowed expanse,
Creatures move softly, lost in their dance.
Life swells around us, in simple delight,
In serenity's arms, the world feels so right.

Shadows lend comfort, the heartbeats align,
Beneath the thick branches, our spirits entwine.
Here in this sanctuary, burdens eclipse,
In the forest canopy, love's quiet script.

With every deep breath, we surrender to peace,
Nature unfolds, and our worries release.
In harmony grounded, together we stand,
In serenity's spell, guided hand in hand.

Embrace of the Evergreen

In the embrace of the evergreen trees,
A whisper of pine dances with ease.
Soft needles descend, a fragrant bed,
In this timeless space, our worries are shed.

Mountains rise high, rugged and grand,
With snow-capped peaks, they patiently stand.
In the shadow of giants, we find our way,
In the embrace of greens, we long to stay.

The cold, crisp air sharpens the mind,
In nature's embrace, true solace we find.
Underneath branches, we cradle our dreams,
Flowing like rivers, reality streams.

The scent of the earth after rain's gentle kiss,
Fills our lungs rich with nature's pure bliss.
In the embrace of the evergreen, we thrive,
In harmony's rhythm, we feel so alive.

With every moment spent, we're forever changed,
Nature's sweet cycles, forever arranged.
Beneath the tall boughs, our spirits have grown,
In the embrace of the trees, we've found our true home.

Boughs and Breezes

Gentle sway of emerald boughs,
Whispers dance upon the breeze.
Nature's song in silent vows,
Calms the heart, puts it at ease.

Rustling leaves a soft embrace,
Cradled in their green expanse.
Time slows down in this sweet space,
Life unfolds in a slow dance.

Birds on high in skies so blue,
Chirping tales of days gone by.
Underneath their watchful view,
We find peace as moments fly.

Sunlight dapples through the trees,
Fleeting shadows play along.
Nature's breath, a gentle tease,
In this place, we all belong.

Every whisper in the air,
Tells a story of its own.
In the boughs, we shed our care,
Amongst the leaves, we have grown.

Solace in the Shade of Evergreens

Underneath the towering pines,
Shadows weave a cool retreat.
Nature's peace in subtle signs,
Comfort dwells where pathways meet.

Whispers cradle in the air,
Softly swaying boughs below.
Time stands still, a tranquil prayer,
Moments pause, and spirits grow.

Green cathedral, vast and wide,
Nurtured by the sun's warm glow.
In this realm, our souls collide,
In the shade, we learn to flow.

Pine-scent lingers in the breeze,
Nature's balm for weary hearts.
Among the roots and rustling leaves,
Renewal blooms as doubt departs.

In the stillness, wisdom reigns,
Echoes of the past resound.
In the shade, we break our chains,
Finding solace all around.

The Pinecone's Silent Lament

Beneath the branches, tales untold,
A pinecone rests, quiet and bold.
Whispers echo through the night,
Memories locked, held tight in plight.

Years have passed, yet still it clings,
To fleeting dreams and fragile things.
In every crack, a story lies,
Of seasons lost and transient skies.

Gentle rains and sunshine's kiss,
Nature's touch brings fleeting bliss.
Yet time, a thief, seeks to remove,
The whispers of what we once loved.

As it waits for winds to call,
And soft embrace before the fall.
Each sigh of breeze, a fond farewell,
A secret wish, a silent spell.

In twilight's glow, it stands alone,
Yearning for the life it's known.
For each pinecone holds the fate,
Of dreams that time cannot abate.

Sunbeams Through Needle Filigree

Sunlight drips through needles fine,
A golden touch on forest floor.
Patterns dance like crafted line,
Where shadows play and spirits soar.

Dappled warmth on mossy beds,
Nature's artwork, pure and true.
Every ray, a story spreads,
Through the green, each life anew.

Flickers spark in emerald hues,
As laughter weaves with rustling leaves.
Amidst the calm, our hearts muse,
In this haven, joy believes.

Branches arch, a grand display,
Framing skies in shifting light.
Nature's canvas, bold and gay,
Painting dreams with sheer delight.

In this place, we find our peace,
Bathed in warmth, our worries cease.
With every beam, a gentle grace,
Life's a dance in this sacred space.

Time's Embrace in the Forest

In the forest's gentle sigh,
Time drifts softly like a dream.
Whispers dance beneath the sky,
Moments flow like a silver stream.

Ancient oaks with tales untold,
Stand as guardians of the past.
Shadows linger, young yet old,
Memories weave, forever cast.

Sunlight dapples on the ground,
Nature hums a lullaby.
Each soft rustle, every sound,
Bears the weight of time gone by.

In the twilight, calm descends,
The world slows into a trance.
Every heartbeat, nature lends,
Life's great rhythm, slow romance.

As stars twinkle through the trees,
Night unveils her velvet cloak.
In the forest's sweet release,
Time's embrace is softly spoke.

Reverie Among the Needle Clusters

Among the needle clusters green,
A dream unfolds in soft retreat.
Whispers echo, barely seen,
Nature's magic, bittersweet.

Sunlight filters through the pine,
Casting shadows, shapes engage.
In this sacred space, divine,
Thoughts unravel, turn the page.

Beneath the branches overhead,
My mind drifts, a gentle stream.
Here, the heart can safely tread,
Lost in wondrous, wild dream.

Each needle, a tale to tell,
Of seasons passed and love once shared.
In this grove, all is well,
Peace encircles, silence spared.

Reveries in fragrant air,
Space to ponder, dwell, reflect.
Among the needles, free from care,
Life's true essence, we protect.

Hibernating in the Hushed Grove

In the hush of winter's reign,
Nature sleeps, a tranquil shroud.
Breath of frost, a silent chain,
Wrapped in white, a gentle cloud.

Branches droop with icy grace,
Covering the world in peace.
Time, a soft and slow embrace,
In the stillness, worries cease.

Beneath the snow, life awaits,
Dreaming dreams in silent dark.
Little hearts, in cozy states,
Hibernating, waiting spark.

Whispers float on winter's breath,
Songs of life, a quiet plea.
In this grove where dreams find death,
Hope unfurls like blooming tree.

When the thaw begins to break,
Life will stir from slumber's hold.
In the hush, it's love we make,
Hibernation, tales retold.

Nature's Resting Whisper

In the meadow, shadows play,
Nature whispers soft and low.
Resting here, I drift away,
In her arms, time moves so slow.

Crickets chirp their lullabies,
Underneath the silver moon.
Stars like diamonds fill the skies,
In the night, all hearts attune.

Flowers close their petals tight,
As the wind begins to sigh.
Though the day fades into night,
Dreams awaken, spirits fly.

Every leaf, a secret kept,
In the stillness, life's embrace.
Nature sings, and softly wept,
Her tranquility, our grace.

With each sigh, the world transforms,
As shadows meld into the dawn.
In her whisper, peace conforms,
Nature's rest, our lives move on.

The Pines Sing Softly

The pines sway gently in the breeze,
Their whispers carried with such ease.
Sunlight filters through the green,
Nature's symphony, calm and serene.

Rustling needles share their cheer,
Echoes weave in the quiet sphere.
A melody of peace unfolds,
In each note, a story told.

Beneath their boughs, the world slows down,
In their embrace, no hint of frown.
The air is thick with scented pine,
A tranquil moment, yours and mine.

Listen closely to the trees,
They sing of secrets, of memories.
A lullaby that never fades,
In woodland depths, the heart invades.

With each soft sigh, the pines will share,
Wisdom found in the open air.
Breathe it in, let worries cease,
In the pines, we find our peace.

The Art of Forest Stillness

Stillness reigns beneath the pines,
In every shade, a tale entwines.
Mossy carpets soft and deep,
Invite the wanderer to keep.

Each sunbeam dances, light and bright,
Illuminating forest's might.
The hush of leaves, the quiet ground,
In stillness, life anew is found.

A heartbeat echoes in the calm,
Nature's rhythm, pure and balm.
Time suspends in tranquil grace,
In these woods, we find our place.

Every breath, a gift so rare,
In the stillness, we find care.
Beneath each branch and azure sky,
The art of forest calls us nigh.

Pause to listen, feel the peace,
As worries fade, and troubles cease.
Within the stillness, life is whole,
A symphony that stirs the soul.

Gentle Whispers Through the Needles

Through the needles, whispers glide,
Secrets of the forest bide.
A gentle rustle, soft and light,
Calls to heart in quiet night.

Each whisper tells of days gone by,
Of soaring birds and a bright sky.
In the breeze, the pines confide,
Fables of the world outside.

Listen close; the needles sway,
As moonlit shadows come to play.
Every murmur drifts like mist,
In nature's arms, you can't resist.

Along the path, the stories brew,
In hints of green and drops of dew.
Nature hums a sacred tune,
While twinkling stars watch from the moon.

Gentle breezes weave their threads,
Carrying whispers from the beds.
Of roots and branches, nightingale,
In needles soft, our dreams set sail.

Moonlight Dancing on Pine Tips

Moonlight spills upon the pines,
Glistening where the shadow twines.
A silver glow, soft and bright,
Dances gently through the night.

Pine tips shimmer like a dream,
Reflecting all in silver gleam.
The night air hums a lullaby,
As constellations float on high.

Whispers of the woodland sigh,
Underneath the starry sky.
In the quiet, hearts will beat,
A rhythmic swell, so smooth and sweet.

Each beam of light a sacred guide,
Through the forest, side by side.
Moonlit paths will lead us home,
In the stillness, we will roam.

As night unfolds, pine fragrance stays,
Wrapping souls in warm embrace.
In the dance of light and shade,
The magic of the night displayed.

Harmonies of Nature's Respite

The sun dips low within the trees,
A gentle breeze hums through the leaves.
Birds sing sweetly, softly calling,
Nature's hymn, a tune enthralling.

Crickets chirp as daylight fades,
In evening's arms, the world invades.
Stars awaken in the sky,
While silent shadows drift on by.

The moonlight weaves through branches bare,
A silver glow beyond compare.
Whispers echo, cool and clear,
Nature's voice, a song sincere.

In this haven, lost in time,
Life unfolds in rhythm and rhyme.
Every moment, softly spun,
A heart at peace, the day is done.

Amidst the stillness, dreams take flight,
In nature's arms, all feels right.
Here, I find my spirit's grace,
In harmony, my sacred space.

A Whispering Haven

Among the trees, where shadows dwell,
The gentle whispers start to swell.
Through branches swayed by softest sighs,
A hidden world beneath the skies.

Flowers bloom, their colors bright,
In morning's glow, they greet the light.
A rustling sound, the leaves take flight,
Caressed by nature's pure delight.

Birds flit by with vibrant grace,
Each melody, a warm embrace.
In quiet corners, secrets hide,
In nature's lap, the heart's abide.

A tranquil brook flows swift and free,
Its laughter weaving harmony.
Where thoughts drift slow like falling leaves,
In whispered peace, my spirit breathes.

This haven calls, a gentle plea,
To linger longer, just to be.
In whispers soft, my soul can mend,
Within this haven, I ascend.

Sanctuary of the Tall Pines

Beneath the boughs of ancient trees,
Where nature sways with timeless ease.
Pines reach high, like watchful eyes,
In their embrace, the spirit flies.

The ground is blanketed in green,
Life's pulse felt in the spaces between.
A hush falls down, the world stands still,
In harmony with nature's will.

With every whisper in the air,
The pinecones drop, a gentle care.
Their fragrance wraps around my soul,
A healing breath that makes me whole.

In the sanctuary, shadows play,
As sunlight dances through the day.
The heartbeats sync with rustling leaves,
In pines' dear arms, the soul believes.

Here solitude finds its grace,
In nature's calm, I find my place.
In this refuge, time stands still,
A sacred bond, a spirit's thrill.

Still Waters of the Woodland Stream

A stream flows gently through the glen,
Mirroring sky where dreams begin.
Cool waters whisper soft and low,
In their embrace, the troubles go.

Pebbles glisten under the sun,
As currents weave and spark their fun.
The world reflects in ripples clear,
A tranquil song for all to hear.

Dragonflies dance upon the breeze,
Their wings aflutter, light with ease.
In this stillness, hearts unite,
With every glance, the world feels right.

Willows droop to kiss the edge,
As nature breathes in softest pledge.
Here, moments linger, melt away,
A memory born in the play.

The woodland stream, a sacred flow,
In quiet strength, its wisdom grows.
Within the stillness, life appears,
In waters deep, I cast my fears.

Milton Keynes UK
Ingram Content Group UK Ltd.
UKHW010232111224
452348UK00011B/699